AN ESSA ON SATIRɛ,
Particularly on the DUNCIAD

By Walter Harte

INTRODUCTION

Since the first publication of Walter Harte's *An Essay on Satire, Particularly on the Dunciad*,[1] it has reappeared more than once: the unsold sheets of the first edition were included in *A Collection of Pieces in Verse and Prose, Which Have Been Publish'd on Occasion of the Dunciad* (1732), and the *Essay* is also found in at least three late eighteenth- or early nineteenth-century collections of poetry.[2] For several reasons, however, it makes sense to reprint the *Essay* again. The three collections are scarce and have forbiddingly small type; I know of no other twentieth-century reprinting; and, perhaps most important, Aubrey Williams claims that "the critical value for the *Dunciad* of Harte's poem has not been fully appreciated."[3] Its value can best be substantiated, or disputed, if it is rescued from its typographical limbo in the collections and reprinted from its more attractive first edition.

Probably the immediate reason for the *Essay* was Harte's admiration for Pope, which arose in part from personal gratitude. On 9 February 1727, Harte wrote an unidentified correspondent that "Mr. Pope was pleased to correct every page" of his forthcoming *Poems on Several Occasions* "with his own hand." Furthermore, Harte may have learned that Pope had petitioned Lady Sarah Cowper, in 1728, to use her influence to obtain him a fellowship in Exeter College, Oxford.[4]

But however appealing the *Essay* may be as an installment on Harte's debt to Pope, there must obviously be better reasons for reprinting it. Harte himself doubtless had additional reasons for writing it. To understand them and the poem, we must also understand, at least in broad outline, the two traditional ways of evaluating satire which Harte and others of his age had inherited. One of them was distinctly at odds with Harte's aims; to the other he gave his support and made his own contribution.

[Pg ii] One tradition stressed the "lowness" of satire, in itself and compared with other genres. This tradition, moreover, had at least two sources: the practice of Elizabethan satirists and the critical custom of assigning satire to a middle or low position in the hierarchy of genres.

From the time of *Piers Plowman*, it was characteristic of English satirists "to taxe the common abuses and vice of the people in rough and bitter speaches."[5] This native character was reenforced by the Elizabethan assumption that there should be similarities between satire and its supposed etymological forebears—the satyrs, legendary half men, half goats of ancient Greece. Believing that the Roman satirists Persius and Juvenal had imitated the uncouth manners and vituperative diction of the satyrs, Elizabethan satirists likewise strove to be as rough, harsh, and licentious as possible.[6] Despite the objections to the satire-satyr etymology stated by Isaac Casaubon,[7] scurrilous satire, especially as a political weapon, was a recognizable subspecies in England at least to 1700. The anonymous author, for instance, of *A Satyr Against Common-Wealths* (1684) contended in his preface that it is "*as disagreeable to see a Satyr Cloath'd in soft and effeminate Language, as to see a Woman scold and vent her self in Billingsgate Rhetorick in a gentile and advantageous Garb.*" But as Harte certainly realized, *The Dunciad* differed greatly from unvarnished abuse, and thus required different standards of critical judgment.

Harte also rejected the critical habit of giving satire a relatively low rank in the scale of literary genres. This habit can be traced to Horace, who belittled the literary status of his own satires,[8] and it was prominent in the Renaissance. The place of satire in a hierarchical list of Julius Caesar Scaliger is perhaps typical: "'And the most noble, of course, are hymns and paeans. In the second place are songs and odes and scolia, which are concerned with the praises of brave men. In the third place the epic, in which there are heroes and other lesser personages. Tragedy together with comedy follows this order; nevertheless comedy will hold the fourth place apart by itself. After these, satires, then exodia, lusus, nuptial songs, elegies, monodia, songs, epigrams.'"[9] Similar rankings of satire frequently recurred in the neo-classical[Pg iii] period,[10] as did the Renaissance supposition that each genre has a style and subject matter appropriate to it. This supposition discouraged any "mixing" of the genres: in Richard Blackmore's words, "all comick Manners, witty Conceits and Ridicule" should be barred from heroic poetry.[11] The influence of the genres theories even after Pope's death may be shown by the fact that Pope, for the very reason that he had failed to work in the major genres, was often ranked below such epic or tragic poets as Spenser, Shakespeare, and Milton.[12]

One senses the foregoing critical assumptions about satire behind much of the early comment on *The Dunciad*. Most of the critics, to be sure, were anything but impartial; in many instances they were smarting from Pope's satire and sought any critical weapons available for retaliation. But it will not do to dismiss these men or their responses to *The Dunciad* as inconsequential; they had the weight of numbers on their side and, more important, the authority of long-established attitudes toward satire.

Although it is frequently impossible to determine exactly which critics Harte was answering in his *Essay*, brief illustration of two prominent types of attack can indicate what he had to vindicate *The Dunciad* against. One of those types resembled Blackmore's objection to a mixing of genres. If satire should be barred from heroic poetry, the reverse, for some critics, was also true, and Pope should not have used epic allusions and devices in *The Dunciad*. Edward Ward, for one, thought the poem an incongruous mixture "against all rule."[13] Pope's violation of "rule" seemed almost a desecration of epic to Thomas Cooke; of the mock-heroic games in Book II of *The Dunciad*, he complained that "to imitate *Virgil* is not to have Games, and those beastly and unnatural, because *Virgil* has noble and reasonable Games, but to preserve a Purity of Manners, Propriety of Conduct founded on Nature, a Beauty and Exactness of Stile, and continued Harmony of Verse concording with the Sense."[14]

The other kind of attack accused Pope of wasting his talents in *The Dunciad*, but palliated blame by reminding him of his demonstrated ability in more worthy poetical pursuits. This was one of[Pg iv] Ward's resources; perhaps disingenuously, he professed amazement that a poet with Pope's "*sublime Genius*," born for "an Epick Muse," "sacred Hymns," and "heav'nly Anthems," would lower himself to mock at "*trifling Foibles*" or "the Starvlings of *Apollo's* Train."[15] More concerned with Pope's potentialities than with his recent ignominy, George Lyttelton nevertheless made essentially the same point: Pope could never become the English Virgil if he "let meaner Satire ... stain the Glory" of his "nobler Lays."[16] And Aaron Hill wrote an allegorical poem to show Pope the error of *The Dunciad* and to suggest means of escape from entombment "in his*own* PROFUND."[17] In such censure we perhaps glimpse an opinion attributable to the still influential genres theories: a poet of "*sublime Genius*" should work in a more sublime poetic genre than satire.

In opposing this low view of satire, Harte drew upon ideas more congenial to his purposes and far more congenial to *The Dunciad*. Originating with the Renaissance commentaries on the formal verse satire of the Romans, their lineage was just as venerable as that of the low view. These critical concepts were probably just as influential too, for they continued to be reiterated by commentaries down to and beyond Pope's time.

Whatever their quarrels, the Renaissance commentaries were virtually united in regarding satire as exalted moral instruction and satirists as ethical philosophers. Casaubon's choice for this sort of praise was Persius; Heinsius and Stapylton likened their respective choices, Horace and Juvenal, to Socrates and Plato; and Rigault considered all three satirists to be philosophers, distinguished only by the different styles which their different periods required. The satirist might disguise himself as a jester, but only to make his moral wisdom more easily digestible; peeling away his mask, "we find in him all the Gods together," "*Maxims or Sentences, that like the lawes of nature, are held sacred by all Nations.*"[18]

Dryden's *Discourse Concerning the Original and Progress of Satire* drew heavily and eclectically upon these commentaries, investing their judgments with a new popularity and authority. Although Dryden condemned Persius for obscurity and other defects,[Pg v] he agreed with Casaubon that Persius excels as a moral philosopher and that "moral doctrine" is more important to satire than wit or urbanity. Dryden knew, moreover, that the satirist's inculcation of "moral doctrine" meant a dual purpose, a pattern of blame and praise—not only "the scourging of vice" but also "exhortation to virtue"—long recognized as a definitive characteristic of formal verse satire.[19] But if Dryden insisted on the moral dignity of satire, he laid equal stress on the dignity attainable through verse and numbers. After complimenting Boileau's *Lutrin* for its successful imitation of Virgil, its blend of "the majesty of the heroic" with the "venom" of satire, Dryden speaks of "the beautiful turns of words and thoughts, which are as requisite in this [satire], as in heroic poetry itself, of which the satire is undoubtedly a species"; and earlier in the *Discourse* he had called heroic poetry "certainly the greatest work of human nature."[20]

It is clear that Harte's *Essay* belongs in the tradition of criticism established by the commentaries on classical satire and continued by Dryden. Like these predecessors, Harte believes that satire is moral philosophy, teaching "the noblest Ethics to reform mankind" (p. 6). Like them again, he believes that to fulfill this purpose satire must not only lash vice but recommend virtue, at least by implication:

Blaspheming *Capaneus* obliquely shows
T'adore those Gods *Aeneas* fears and knows, (p. 10)[21]

But perhaps Harte's overriding concern was to do for satire (with *The Dunciad* as his focus) what Dryden's *Discourse* had done: to reassert its dignity and majesty.

Although Harte is quite careful to distinguish satire from epic poetry, the total effect of his *Essay* is to blur this distinction and to raise *The Dunciad* very nearly to the level of genuine epic. The term "*Epic Satire*" (p. 6) certainly seems to refer to the wedding of two disparate genres in *The Dunciad*, lifting it above satire that is merely "rugged" or "mischievously gay" (p. 8). (The epithet is also, perhaps, a thrust at Edward Ward, who had pinned it on *The Dunciad* with a sneer.)[22] Harte's claim that

[Pg vi]*Books and the Man* demands as much, or more,
Than *He who wander'd to the Latian shore* (p. 9)

has a similar effect. The greatest epic poets and satirists have always transcended rules to follow "Nature's light"; Pope, over-topping them all, has "still corrected Nature as she stray'd" (pp. 19, 21). But perhaps Harte's most successful attempt to elevate *The Dunciad* comes in section two of his poem. Unlike Dryden, in whose *Discourse* the account of the "progress" of satire is confined almost exclusively to a few Roman writers, Harte begins his account of its progress with Homer and brings it down to Pope. Deriving the ancestry of *The Dunciad* from Homer, the greatest epic poet, obviously enhances Pope's satire. Perhaps less obviously, by extending Dryden's account to the present, Harte makes *The Dunciad* not only a chronological *terminus ad quem* but, far more important, the fruit of centuries of slowly accumulating mastery and wisdom.

The strategies mentioned thus far constitute one series of answers to critics who charged Pope with debasing true epic. But Harte also addressed himself to such critics more directly. Although Aubrey Williams (p. 54) has clearly demonstrated Harte's awareness that the world of *The Dunciad* does in one sense sully epic beauties, at the same time, I think, Harte knew that the epic poems to which *The Dunciad* continually alludes remain fixed, unsullied polestars; otherwise the reader of the poem would lack a way of measuring the meanness of its characters and principles. The "charms of *Parody*" in *The Dunciad* provide a contrast between its dark, fallen world and the undimmed luster of epic realms (p. 10). By using the ambiguous word *parody*, which in the eighteenth century could mean either ridicule or straight imitation,[23] Harte skillfully suggests the complex purpose of Pope's epic backdrop. The dunces, not Pope, ridicule the epic world by their words and deeds; but in turn, this world ridicules them simply by being "imitated" and incorporated in *The Dunciad*. And its incorporation is by no means equivalent to the pollution of epic. That, Harte hints, is the achievement of scribblers like Blackmore (p. 12). It is they who inadvertently write mock-epics, parodies which degrade their[Pg vii] great models; Pope, nominally writing mock-epic, actually approaches epic achievement.

Harte's reply to those who believed Pope had wasted his talent in attacking "the Refuse of the Town" centers in the stanza beginning on p. 24 but can be found elsewhere as well. Literary "Refuse," he realized, could not safely be ignored, for he at least came close to understanding that it was "the metaphor by which bigger deteriorations," social and moral, "are revealed" (Williams, p. 14).

... Rules, and Truth, and Order, Dunces strike;
Of Arts, and Virtues, enemies alike. (p. 24)

Ultimately, then, Harte seemed aware that the dunces pose a colossal threat, a threat which warrants Pope's numerous echoes of *Paradise Lost*. Harte's *Essay*, in fact, contains several echoes of the same poem. Though, like most of Pope's, these Miltonic echoes are given a comic turn which indicates a wide gap between the real satanic host and its London auxiliary, there is little doubt that Harte grasped the underlying seriousness of his mentor's analogies and his own.

A few words remain to be said about Boileau's *Discourse of Satires Arraigning Persons by Name*, which so far as I know appeared with all early printings of Harte's *Essay*.

The *Discourse* was first published in 1668, with the separately printed edition of Boileau's ninth satire; in the same year it was included in a collected edition of the satires. It was occasioned, evidently, by a critic's complaint that the modern satirist, departing from ancient practice, "offers insults to individuals."[24]

The only English translation of the *Discourse* that I have discovered before 1730 appears in volume two (1711) of a three-volume translation of Boileau's works. This, however, is not the same translation as the one accompanying Harte's *Essay*; it is noticeably less fluent and lacks (as does the French) the subtitle "arraigning persons by name."

The 1730 translation is faithful to the original, and the subtitle[Pg viii] calls attention to the aptness of the *Discourse* as a defense of Pope's satiric practice.[25] It is so apt, indeed, that one could almost suspect Pope himself of making the translation and submitting it to Harte or his publisher. Pope had already invoked Boileau's name and precedent in the letter from "William Cleland"; nothing could be more logical than for Pope to turn the esteemed Boileau's self-justification to his own ends.

Cornell College

[Pg ix]

NOTES TO THE INTRODUCTION

[1] Robert W. Rogers, *The Major Satires of Alexander Pope*, Illinois Studies in Language and Literature, XL (Urbana, 1955), p. 140, dates the Essay January 7-14, 1731, N. S., on the evidence of *The Grub-Street Journal*; No. 484 of *The London Evening-Post* (Saturday, January 9, to Tuesday, January 12, 1731) advertises its publication for the following day.

[2] Rogers, p. 141. Thomas Park, *Supplement to the British Poets* (London, 1809), VIII, 21-36; Alexander Chalmers, *The Works of the English Poets* (London, 1810), XVI, 348-352; Robert Anderson, *A Complete Edition of the Poets of Great Britain* (London, 1794), IX, 825-982 [*sic*].

[3] *Pope's "Dunciad": A Study of Its Meaning* (Baton Rouge, 1955), p. 54n.

[4] *The Correspondence of Alexander Pope*, ed. George Sherburn (Oxford, 1956), II, 430 n., 497.

[5] George Puttenham, *The Arte of English Poesie* (1589), in *Elizabethan Critical Essays*, ed. G. Gregory Smith (Oxford, 1904), II, 27.

[6] Alvin Kernan, *The Cankered Muse: Satire of the English Renaissance*, Yale Studies in English, CXLII (New Haven, 1959), pp. 55, 58, 62; Oscar James Campbell, *Comicall Satyre and Shakespeare's "Troilus and Cressida"* (San Marino, 1959), pp. 24-25, 27, 29-30.

[7] *De Satyrica Graecorum Poesi, & Romanorum Satira Libri Duo* (Paris, 1605).

[8] J. F. D'Alton, *Roman Literary Theory and Criticism: A Study in Tendencies* (London, New York, and Toronto, 1931), pp. 356, 414 and n.; George Converse Fiske, *Lucilius and Horace: A Study in the Classical Theory of Imitation*, University of Wisconsin Studies in Language and Literature, No. 7 (Madison, 1920), p. 443.

[9] Bernard Weinberg, *A History of Literary Criticism in the Italian Renaissance*(Chicago, 1961), II, 745. For similar appraisals of satire, see also I, 148-149; II, 759, 807; and Puttenham, pp. 26-28.

[Pg x][10] E.g., John Dennis, "The Grounds of Criticism in Poetry" (1704), in *The Critical Works*, ed. Edward Niles Hooker (Baltimore, 1939-1943), I, 338; Joseph Trapp, *Lectures on Poetry Read in the Schools of Natural Philsophy at Oxford* (London, 1742), p. 153.

[11] *Essays upon Several Subjects* (London, 1716-1717), I, 76.

[12] Paul F. Leedy, "Genres Criticism and the Significance of Warton's Essay on Pope,"*JEGP*, XLV (1946), 141.

[13] *Durgen. Or, A Plain Satyr upon a Pompous Satyrist* (London, 1729), p. 48.

[14] "The Battel of the Poets," in *Tales, Epistles, Odes, Fables, etc.* (London, 1729), p. 138n. Though the poem was first published in 1725, it was revised to attack *The Dunciad*; Cooke claims ("The Preface," p. 107) that not more than eighty lines in the two versions are the same.

[15] *Durgen*, pp. [i], 19, 40-41.

[16] *An Epistle to Mr. Pope, from a Young Gentleman at Rome* (London, 1730), pp. 6-7.

[17] *The Progress of Wit* (London, 1730), p. 31. Two months after Harte's Essay appeared Hill's *Advice to the Poets*, which complements the earlier allegory by urging Pope to shun "*vulgar Genii*" and emulate "Thy own *Ulysses*" (pp. 18-19).

[18] Daniel Heinsius, "De Satyra Horatiana Liber," in *Q. Horati Flacci Opera* (1612), pp. 137-138; Sir Robert Stapylton, "The Life and Character of Juvenal," in *Mores Hominum. The Manners of Men, Described in Sixteen Satyrs, by Juvenal* (London, 1660), p. [v]; Nicolas Rigault, "De Satira Juvenalis Dissertatio" (1615), in *Decii Junii Juvenalis Satirarum Libri Quinque* (Paris, 1754), p. xxv; and André Dacier, *An Essay upon Satyr* (London, 1695), p. 273.

[19] *Essays of John Dryden*, ed. W. P. Ker (Oxford, 1900), II, 75, 104-105; Howard D. Weinbrot, "The Pattern of Formal Verse Satire in the Restoration and the Eighteenth Century," *PMLA*, LXXX (1965), 394-401; Causaubon, *De Satyrica Graecorum Poesi, & Romanorum Satira Libri Duo*, pp. 291-292; Heinsius, pp. 137-138.

[20] *Essays*, II, 43, 107-108.

[21] See Weinbrot, p. 399.

[Pg xi][22] *Durgen*, p. 3.

[23] Howard D. Weinbrot, "Parody as Imitation in the 18th Century," *AN&Q*, II (1964), 131-134.

[24] Boileau, *Oeuvres Complètes*, ed. Françoise Escal (Éditions Gallimard, 1966), p. 924.

[25] Numerous protests against Pope's use of names made such a defense desirable. See, for example, Ward (p. 9) and "A Letter to a Noble Lord: Occasion'd by the Late Publication of the Dunciad Variorum," in *Pope Alexander's Supremacy and Infallibility Examin'd* (London, 1729), p. 12. Boileau's *Discourse* is a particularly apposite reply to the latter, which had contrasted Pope's satiric practice with that of Horace, Juvenal, and Boileau.

BIBLIOGRAPHICAL NOTE

The text of this edition is reproduced from a copy in the University of Illinois Library.

**AN
ESSAY
ON
SATIRE,
Particularly on the DUNCIAD.**

(Price One Shilling.)

Speedily will be Published,

The Works
of VIRGIL Translated
into Blank Verse by *J. Trapp*, D. D.
in Three Volumes in 12° with Cuts.

**AN
ESSAY**

6

ON
SATIRE,
Particularly on the
DUNCIAD.

BY
Mr. *WALTER HARTE*
of St. *Mary-Hall*, Oxon.

To which is added, A
DISCOURSE *on* SATIRES,
Arraigning Persons by Name.
By Monsieur BOILEAU.

LONDON:
Printed for LAWTON GILLIVER at *Homer's* Head
against St. *Dunstan's* Church, in *Fleetstreet*,
MDCCXXX.

THE
CONTENTS.

[Pg 5]

An

7

ESSAY
ON
SATIRE.

T' Exalt the Soul, or make the Heart sincere,
To arm our Lives with honesty severe,
To shake the wretch beyond the reach of Law,
Deter the young, and touch the bold with awe,
To raise the fal'n, to hear the sufferer's cries,
[Pg 6]And sanctify the virtues of the wise,
Old Satire rose from Probity of mind,
The noblest Ethicks to reform mankind.

As *Cynthia's* Orb excels the gems of night:
So *Epic Satire* shines distinctly bright.
Here Genius lives, and strength in every part,
And lights and shades, and fancy fix'd by art.
A second beauty in its nature lies,
It gives not *Things*, but *Beings* to our eyes,
Life, *Substance*, *Spirit* animate the whole;
Fiction and *Fable* are the Sense and Soul.
The *common Dulness* of mankind, array'd
In pomp, here lives and breathes, a *wond'rous Maid*:
The Poet decks her with each unknown Grace,
Clears her dull brain, and brightens her dark face:
See! Father *Chaos* o'er his First-born nods,
[Pg 7]And Mother *Night*, in Majesty of Gods!
See *Querno's Throne*, by hands Pontific rise,
And a *Fool's Pandæmonium* strike our Eyes!
Ev'n what on C——l the Publick bounteous pours,
Is sublimated here to *Golden show'rs*.

A *Dunciad* or a *Lutrin* is compleat,
And *one* in action; ludicrously great.
Each wheel rolls round in due degrees of force;
E'en *Episodes* are *needful*, or *of course*:
Of course, when things are virtually begun
E'er the first ends, the Father and the Son:
Or else so *needful*, and exactly grac'd,
That nothing is *ill-suited*, or *ill-plac'd*.

True Epic's a vast World, and this a small;
One has its *proper* beauties, and one *all*.
[Pg 8]Like *Cynthia*, one in *thirty days* appears,
Like *Saturn* one, rolls round in *thirty years*.
There opens a wide Tract, a length of Floods,
A height of Mountains, and a waste of Woods:
Here but one Spot; nor Leaf, nor Green depart
From Rules, e'en Nature seems the Child of Art.
As *Unities* in Epick works appear,

8

So must they shine in full distinction here.
Ev'n the warm *Iliad* moves with slower pow'rs:
That forty days demands, This forty hours.

Each other Satire humbler arts has known,
Content with meaner Beauties, tho' its own:
Enough for that, if rugged in its course
The Verse but rolls with Vehemence and Force;
Or nicely pointed in th' *Horatian* way
[Pg 9]Wounds keen, like *Syrens* mischievously gay.
Here, All has *Wit*, yet must that Wit be *strong*,
Beyond the Turns of *Epigram*, or *Song*.
The *Thought* must rise exactly from the vice,
Sudden, yet *finish'd*, *clear*, and yet *concise*.
One Harmony must *first* with *last* unite;
As all true Paintings have their *Place* and *Light*.
Transitions must be *quick*, and yet *design'd*,
Not made to fill, but just retain the mind:
And *Similies*, like meteors of the night,
Just give one flash of momentary Light.

As thinking makes the Soul, low things exprest
In high-rais'd terms, define a *Dunciad* best.
Books and the Man demands as much, or more,
Than *He* who *wander'd to the Latian Shore*:
For here (eternal Grief to *Duns*'s soul,
And *B*——'s thin Ghost!) the *Part* contains the *Whole*:
[Pg 10]Since in Mock-Epic none succeeds, but he
Who tastes the Whole of Epic Poesy.

The *Moral* must be clear and understood;
But finer still, if negatively good:
Blaspheming *Capaneus* obliquely shows
T' adore those Gods *Æneas* fears and knows.
A *Fool's* the *Heroe*; but the *Poet's* end
Is, to be *candid*, *modest*, and a *Friend*.

Let *Classic Learning* sanctify each Part,
Not only show your Reading, but your Art.

The charms of *Parody*, like those of Wit,
If well *contrasted*, never fail to hit;
One half in light, and one in darkness drest,
(For contraries oppos'd still shine the best.)
[Pg 11]When a cold Page half breaks the Writer's heart,
By this it warms, and brightens into Art.
When Rhet'ric glitters with too pompous pride,
By this, like *Circe*, 'tis un-deify'd.
So *Berecynthia*, while her off-spring vye

In homage to the Mother of the sky,
(Deck'd in rich robes, of trees, and plants, and flow'rs,
And crown'd illustrious with an hundred tow'rs)
O'er all *Parnassus* casts her eyes at once,
And sees an hundred Sons—*and each a Dunce.*

The *Language* next: from hence new pleasure springs;
For *Styles* are dignify'd, as well as *Things.*
Tho' Sense subsists, distinct from phrase or sound,
Yet *Gravity* conveys a surer wound.
[Pg 12]The chymic secret which your pains wou'd find,
Breaks out, unsought for, in *Cervantes'* mind;
And *Quixot's* wildness, like that King's of old,
Turns all he touches, into *Pomp* and *Gold.*
Yet in this Pomp discretion must be had;
Tho' *grave,* not *stiff*; tho' *whimsical,* not *mad*:
In Works like these if *Fustian* might appear,
Mock-Epics, *Blackmore,* would not cost thee dear.

We grant, that *Butler* ravishes the Heart,
As *Shakespear* soar'd beyond the reach of Art;
(For Nature form'd those Poets without Rules,
To fill the world with *imitating Fools.*)
What *Burlesque* could, was by that Genius done;
Yet faults it has, impossible to shun:
Th' unchanging strain for want of grandeur cloys,
And gives too oft the horse-laugh mirth of Boys:
[Pg 13]The short-legg'd verse, and double-gingling Sound,
So quick surprize us, that our heads run round:
Yet in this Work peculiar Life presides,
And *Wit,* for all the world to glean besides.

Here pause, my Muse, too daring and too young!
Nor rashly aim at Precepts yet unsung.
Can Man the Master of the *Dunciad* teach?
And these new Bays what other hopes to reach?
'Twere better judg'd, to study and explain
Each ancient Grace he copies not in vain;
To trace thee, Satire, to thy utmost Spring,
Thy Form, thy Changes, and thy Authors sing.

All Nations with this Liberty dispense,
[Pg 14]And bid us shock the Man that shocks Good Sense.
Great *Homer* first the Mimic Sketch design'd
What grasp'd not *Homer's* comprehensive mind?
By him who *Virtue* prais'd, was *Folly* curst,
And who *Achilles* sung, drew *Dunce the First.*[26]

Next him *Simonides,* with lighter Air,

In Beasts, and Apes, and Vermin, paints the *Fair*.
The good *Scriblerus* in like forms displays
The reptile Rhimesters of these later days.

More fierce, *Archilochus*! thy vengeful flame;
Fools read and *dy'd*: for Blockheads then had *Shame*.

The Comic-Satirist[27] attack'd his Age,
[Pg 15]And found low Arts, and Pride, among the Sage:
See learned *Athens* stand attentive by,
And *Stoicks* learn their Foibles from the Eye.

Latium's fifth Homer[28] held the *Greeks* in view;
Solid, tho' rough, yet incorrect as new.
Lucilius, warm'd with more than mortal flame
Rose next[29], and held a torch to ev'ry shame.
See stern *Menippus*, cynical, unclean;
And *Grecian Cento*'s, mannerly obscene.
Add the last efforts of *Pacuvius'* rage,
And the chaste decency of *Varro*'s page.[30]

See *Horace* next, in each reflection nice,
Learn'd, but not vain, the Foe of Fools nor Vice.
Each page instructs, each Sentiment prevails,
All shines alike, he rallies, but ne'er rails:
[Pg 16]With courtly ease conceals a Master's art,
And least-expected steals upon the heart.
Yet *Cassius*[31] felt the fury of his rage,
(*Cassius*, the *We——d* of a former age)
And sad *Alpinus*, ignorantly read,
Who murder'd *Memnon*, tho' for ages dead.

Then *Persius* came: whose line tho' roughly wrought,
His Sense o'erpaid the stricture of his thought.
Here in clear light the *Stoic*-doctrine shines,
Truth all subdues, or Patience all resigns.
A Mind supreme![32] impartial, yet severe:
Pure in each Act, in each Recess sincere!
Yet *rich ill* Poets urg'd the *Stoic*'s Frown,
And bade him strike at *Dulness* and a *Crown*.[33]
[Pg 17]
The Vice and Luxury *Petronius* drew,
In *Nero* meet: th' imperial point of view:
The Roman *Wilmot*, that could Vice chastize,
Pleas'd the mad King he serv'd, to satirize.

The next[34] in Satire felt a nobler rage,
What honest Heart could bear *Domitian*'s age?
See his strong Sense, and Numbers masculine!

11

His Soul is kindled, and he kindles mine:
Scornful of Vice, and fearless of Offence,
He flows a Torrent of impetuous Sense.

Lo! Savage Tyrants Who blasphem'd their God
Turn Suppliants now, and gaze at *Julian*'s Rod.[35]
[Pg 18]
Lucian, severe, but in a gay disguise,
Attacks old Faith, or sports in learned Lyes;[36]
Sets Heroes and Philosophers at odds;
And scourges Mortals, and dethrones the Gods.

Then all was Night—But *Satire* rose once more
Where *Medici* and *Leo* Arts restore.
Tassonè shone fantastic, but sublime:
And He, who form'd the *Macaronique*-Rhime:

Then *Westward* too by slow degrees confest,
Where boundless *Rabelais* made the World his Jest;
Marot had Nature, *Regnier* Force and Flame,
But swallow'd all in *Boileau*'s matchless Fame!
Extensive Soul! who rang'd all learning o'er,
Present and past—and yet found room for more.
[Pg 19]Full of new Sense, exact in every Page,
Unbounded, and yet sober in thy Rage.
Strange Fate! *Thy solid* Sterling *of two lines,*
Drawn to our Tinsel, *thro' whole Pages shines!*[37]

In *Albion* then, with equal lustre bright,
Great *Dryden* rose, and steer'd by Nature's light.
Two glimmering Orbs he just observ'd from far,
The Ocean wide, and dubious either Star,
Donne teem'd with Wit, but all was maim'd and bruis'd,
The periods endless, and the sense confus'd:
Oldham rush'd on, impetuous, and sublime,
But lame in Language, Harmony, and Rhyme;
These (with new graces) vig'rous nature join'd
In one, and center'd 'em in *Dryden*'s mind.
[Pg 20]How full thy verse? Thy meaning how severe?
How dark thy theme? yet made exactly clear.
Not mortal is thy accent, nor thy rage,
Yet mercy softens, or contracts each Page.
Dread Bard! instruct us to revere thy rules,
And hate like thee, all Rebels, and all Fools.

His Spirit ceas'd not (in strict truth) to be;
For dying *Dryden* breath'd, O *Garth!* on thee,
Bade thee to keep alive his genuine Rage,
Half-sunk in want, oppression and old age;

12

Then, when thy pious hands repos'd his head,[38]
When vain young Lords and ev'n the Flamen fled.
For well thou knew'st his merit and his art,
His upright mind, clear head, and friendly heart.
[Pg 21]Ev'n *Pope* himself (who sees no Virtue bleed
But bears th' affliction) envies thee the deed.

O *Pope*! Instructor of my studious days,
Who fix'd my steps in virtue's early ways:
On whom our labours, and our hopes depend,
Thou more than Patron, and ev'n more than Friend!
Above all Flattery, all Thirst of Gain,
And Mortal but in Sickness, and in Pain!
Thou taught'st old Satire nobler fruits to bear,
And check'd her Licence with a moral Care:
Thou gav'st the Thought new beauties not its own,
And touch'd the Verse with Graces yet unknown.
Each lawless branch thy level eye survey'd.
And still corrected Nature as she stray'd:
Warm'd *Boileau*'s Sense with *Britain*'s genuine Fire,
And added Softness to *Tassone*'s Lyre.
[Pg 22]
Yet mark the hideous nonsense of the age,
And thou thy self the subject of its rage.
So in old times, round godlike *Scæva* ran
Rome's dastard Sons, a *Million*, and a *Man*.

Th' exalted merits of the Wise and Good
Are seen, far off, and rarely understood.
The world's a father to a Dunce unknown,
And much he thrives, for Dulness! he's thy own.
No hackney brethren e'er condemn him *twice*;
He fears no enemies, but dust and mice.

If *Pope* but writes, the Devil *Legion* raves,
And meagre Critics mutter in their caves:
(Such Critics of necessity consume
All Wit, as Hangmen ravish'd Maids at *Rome*.)
Names he a Scribler? all the world's in arms,
Augusta, Granta, Rhedecyna swarms:
[Pg 23]The guilty reader fancies what he fears,
And every *Midas* trembles for his ears.

See all such malice, obloquy, and spite
Expire e're morn, the mushroom of a night!
Transient as vapours glimm'ring thro' the glades,
Half-form'd and idle, as the dreams of maids,
Vain as the sick man's vow, or young man's sigh,
Third-nights of Bards, or *H———*'s sophistry.

13

These ever hate the Poet's sacred line:
These hate whate'er is glorious, or divine.
From one Eternal Fountain *Beauty* springs,
The Energy of *Wit*, and *Truth of Things*,
That Source is GOD: From *him* they downwards tend,
Flow round—yet in their native center end.
[Pg 24]Hence Rules, and Truth, and Order, Dunces strike;
Of Arts, and Virtues, enemies alike.

Some urge, that Poets of supreme renown
Judge ill to scourge the Refuse of the Town.
How'ere their Casuists hope to turn the scale,
These men must smart, or scandal will prevail.
By these, the weaker Sex still suffer most:
And such are prais'd who rose at Honour's cost:
The Learn'd they wound, the Virtuous, and the Fair,
No fault they cancel, no reproach they spare:
The random Shaft, impetuous in the dark,
Sings on unseen, and quivers in the mark.
'Tis Justice, and not Anger, makes us write,
Such sons of darkness must be drag'd to light:
Long-suff'ring nature must not always hold;
In virtue's cause 'tis gen'rous to be bold.
[Pg 25]To scourge the bad, th' unwary to reclaim,
And make light flash upon the face of shame.

Others have urg'd (but weigh it, and you'll find
'Tis light as feathers blown before the wind)
That Poverty, the Curse of Providence,
Attones for a dull Writer's want of Sense:
Alas! his Dulness 'twas that made him poor;
Not *vice versa*: We infer no more.
Of Vice and Folly Poverty's the curse,
Heav'n may be rigid, but the Man was worse,
By good made bad, by favours more disgrac'd,
So dire th' effects of ignorance misplac'd!
Of idle Youth, unwatch'd by Parents eyes!
Of Zeal for pence, and Dedication Lies!
Of conscience model'd by a Great man's looks!
And arguings in religion—from No books!
[Pg 26]
No light the darkness of that mind invades,
Where *Chaos* rules, enshrin'd in genuine Shades;
Where, in the Dungeon of the Soul inclos'd,
True Dulness nods, reclining and repos'd.
Sense, Grace, or Harmony, ne'er enter there,
Nor human Faith, nor Piety sincere;
A mid-night of the Spirits, Soul, and Head,

14

(Suspended all) as Thought it self lay dead.
Yet oft a mimic gleam of transient light
Breaks thro' this gloom, and then they think they write;
From Streets to Streets th' unnumber'd Pamphlets fly,
Then tremble *Warner*, *Brown*, and *Billingsly*.[39]
[Pg 27]
O thou most gentle Deity appear,
Thou who still hear'st, and yet art prone to hear:
Whose eye ne'er closes, and whose brains ne'er rest,
(Thy own dear Dulness bawling at thy breast)
Attend, O *Patience*, on thy arm reclin'd,
And see Wit's endless enemies behind!

And ye, *Our Muses*, with a *hundred tongues*,
And Thou, O *Henley!* blest with *brazen lungs*;
Fanatic *Withers!* fam'd for rhimes and sighs,
And *Jacob Behmen!* most obscurely wise;
From darkness palpable, on dusky wings
Ascend! and shroud him who your Off-spring sings.

The first with *Egypt*'s darkness in his head
Thinks Wit the devil, and curses books unread.
[Pg 28]For twice ten winters has he blunder'd on,
Thro' heavy comments, yet ne'er lost nor won:
Much may be done in twenty winters more,
And let him then learn *English* at threescore.
No sacred *Maro* glitters on his shelf,
He wants the mighty *Stagyrite* himself.
See vast *Coimbria*'s comments[40] pil'd on high,
In heaps *Soncinas*,[41] *Sotus*, *Sanchez* lie:
For idle hours, *Sà*'s[42] idler casuistry.

Yet worse is he, who in one language read,
Has one eternal jingling in his head,
At night, at morn, in bed, and on the stairs ...
Talks flights to grooms, and makes lewd songs at pray'rs
[Pg 29]His Pride, a Pun: a Guinea his Reward,
His Critick *G-ld-n*, *Jemmy M-re* his Bard.

What artful Hand the Wretch's Form can hit,
Begot by *Satan* on a *M———ly*'s Wit:
In Parties furious at the great Man's nod,
And hating none for nothing, but his God:
Foe to the Learn'd, the Virtuous, and the Sage,
A Pimp in Youth, an Atheist in old Age:
Now plung'd in Bawdry and substantial Lyes,
Now dab'ling in ungodly Theories;
But so, as Swallows skim the pleasing flood,
Grows giddy, but ne'er drinks to do him good:

15

Alike resolv'd to flatter, or to cheat,
Nay worship Onions, if they cry, *come eat*:
A foe to Faith, in Revelation blind,
And impious much, as Dunces are by kind.
[Pg 30]
Next see the Master-piece of Flatt'ry rise,
Th' anointed Son of Dulness and of Lies:
Whose softest Whisper fills a Patron's Ear,
Who smiles unpleas'd, and mourns without a tear.[43]
Persuasive, tho' a woful Blockhead he:
Truth dies before his shadowy Sophistry.
For well he knows[44] the Vices of the Town,
The Schemes of State, and Int'rest of the Gown;
Immoral Afternoons, indecent Nights,
Enflaming Wines, and second Appetites.
[Pg 31]
But most the Theatres with dulness groan,
Embrio's half-form'd, a Progeny unknown:
Fine things for nothing, transports out of season,
Effects un-caus'd, and murders without reason.
Here Worlds run round, and Years are taught to stay,
Each Scene an Elegy, each Act a Play.[45]
Can the same Pow'r such various Passions move?
Rejoice, or weep, 'tis ev'ry thing for *Love*.
The self-same Cause produces Heav'n and Hell:
Things contrary as Buckets in a Well;
One up, one down, one empty, and one full:
Half high, half low, half witty, and half dull.
So on the borders of an ancient Wood,
Or where some Poplar trembles o'er the Flood,
[Pg 32]*Arachnè* travels on her filmy thread,
Now high, now low, or on her feet or head.

Yet these love Verse, as Croaking comforts Frogs,[46]
And Mire and Ordure are the Heav'n of Hogs.
As well might Nothing bind Immensity,
Or passive Matter Immaterials see,
As these shou'd write by reason, rhime, and rule,
Or we turn Wit, whom nature doom'd a Fool.
If *Dryden* err'd, 'twas human frailty once,
But blund'ring is the Essence of a Dunce.
[Pg 33]
Some write for Glory, but the Phantom fades;
Some write as Party, or as Spleen invades;
A third, because his Father was well read,
And Murd'rer-like, calls Blushes from the dead.
Yet all for Morals and for Arts contend——
They want 'em both, who never prais'd a Friend.
More ill, than dull; For pure stupidity

Was ne'er a crime in honest *Banks*, or me.

See next a Croud in damasks, silks, and crapes,
Equivocal in dress, half-belles, half-trapes:
A length of night-gown rich *Phantasia* trails,
Olinda wears one shift, and pares no nails:
Some in C——*l*'s Cabinet each act display,
When nature in a transport dies away:
[Pg 34]Some more refin'd transcribe their Opera-loves
On Iv'ry Tablets, or in clean white Gloves:
Some of Platonic, some of carnal Taste,
Hoop'd, or un-hoop'd, ungarter'd, or unlac'd.
Thus thick in Air the wing'd Creation play,
When vernal *Phœbus* rouls the Light away,
A motley race, half Insects and half Fowls,
Loose-tail'd and dirty, May-flies, Bats, and Owls.

Gods, that this native nonsense was our worst!
With Crimes more deep, O *Albion!* art thou curst.
No Judgment open Prophanation fears,
For who dreads God, that can preserve his Ears?
Oh save me Providence, from Vice refin'd,
That worst of ills, a *Speculative Mind*[47]
[Pg 35]Not that I blame divine Philosophy,
(Yet much we risque, for Pride and Learning lye.)
Heav'n's paths are found by Nature more than Art,
The Schoolman's Head misleads the Layman's Heart.

What unrepented Deeds has *Albion* done?
Yet spare us Heav'n! return, and spare thy own.
Religion vanishes to *Types*, and *Shade*,
By Wits, by fools, by her own Sons betray'd!
Sure 'twas enough to give the Dev'l his due,
Must such Men mingle with the *Priesthood* too?
So stood *Onias* at th' Almighty's Throne,
Profanely cinctur'd in a Harlot's Zone.

Some *Rome*, and some the *Reformation* blame;
'Tis hard to say from whence such License came;
[Pg 36]From fierce Enthusiasts, or Socinians sad?
C————*ns* the soft, or *Bourignon* the mad?
From wayward Nature, or lewd Poet's Rhimes?
From praying, canting, or king-killing times?
From all the dregs which *Gallia* cou'd pour forth,
(Those Sons of Schism) landed in the *North?*—
From whence it came, they and the D——l best know,
Yet thus much, *Pope*, each Atheist is thy Foe.

O Decency, forgive these friendly Rhimes,

For raking in the dunghill of their crimes.
To name each Monster wou'd make Printing dear,
Or tire *Ned Ward*, who writes six Books a-year.
Such vicious Nonsense, Impudence, and Spite,
Wou'd make a Hermit, or a Father write.
[Pg 37]Tho' *Julian* rul'd the World, and held no more
Than deist *Gildon* taught, or *Toland* swore,
Good *Greg'ry*[48] prov'd him execrably bad,
And scourg'd his Soul, with drunken Reason mad.
Much longer, *Pope* restrain'd his awful hand,
Wept o'er poor *Niniveh*, and her dull band,
'Till Fools like Weeds rose up, and choak'd the Land.
Long, long he slumber'd e'er th' avenging hour;
For dubious Mercy half o'er-rul'd his pow'r:
'Till the wing'd bolt, red-hissing from above
Pierc'd Millions thro'——For such the Wrath of *Jove*.
Hell, Chaos, Darkness, tremble at the sound,
And prostrate Fools bestrow the vast Profound:
[Pg 38]No *Charon* wafts 'em from the farther Shore,
Silent they sleep, alas! to rise no more.

Oh POPE, and Sacred *Criticism!* forgive
A Youth, who dares approach your Shrine, and live!
Far has he wander'd in an unknown Night,
No Guide to lead him, but his own dim Light.
For him more fit, in vulgar Paths to tread,
To shew th' Unlearned what they never read,
Youth to improve, or rising Genius tend,
To Science much, to Virtue more, a Friend.

Footnotes:

[26] Margites.
[27] Aristophanes.
[28] Ennius.
[29] ——clarumq; facem præferre pudori, *Juv. S*. 1.
[30] *See* Varro's *Character in* Cicero's *Academics.*
[31] *Epode* 6.
[32] *Alludes to this Couplet in his second Satire,*

Compositum jus fasq; animi, sanctiq; recessus,
Mentis, & incoctum generoso pectus honesto.

[33] *See his first Satire of* Nero's *Verses,* &c.
[34] Juvenal.

[35] *The* Cæsars *of the Emperor* Julian.

[36] Lucian*'s True History.*

[37] Roscommon, *Revers'd.*

[38] *Dr.* Garth *took care of Mr.* Dryden*'s Funeral, which some Noblemen, who undertook it, had neglected.*

[39] Three Booksellers.

[40] Coimbria*'s comments.* Colleg. Conimbricense, *a Society in* Spain, *which publish'd tedious explanations of* Aristotle.

[41] Soncinas, *a Schoolman.*

[42] Sa (Eman. de) *See* Paschal*'s Mystery of Jesuitism.*

[43]

Pompeius, tenui jugulos aperire susurro. Juv. S. 4.

Flet, si lacrymas aspexit amici, Nec dolet. S. 3.

[44]

——Noverat ille

Luxuriam Imperii veteris, noctesq; Neronis

Jam medias, aliamq; famem. Juv. S. 4.

[45] Et chaque Acte en fa pièce & una pièce entière. *Boil.*

[46] *'When a poor Genius has labour'd much, he judges well not to expect the Encomiums of the Publick: for these are not his due. Yet for fear his drudgery shou'd have no recompense, God (of his goodness) has given him a personal Satisfaction. To envy him in this wou'd be injustice beyond barbarity itself: Thus the same Deity (who is equally just in all points) has given Frogs the comfort of Croaking,* &c

Le Pere Gerasse Sommes Theol. L. 2.

[47] Plato *calls this an Ignorance of a dark and dangerous Nature, under appearance of the greatest Wisdom.*

[48] Gregory Nazianz: *a Father at the beginning of the Fourth Century. He writ two most bitter Satires (or Invectives) against the Emperor* Julian.

[Pg 39]

A
DISCOURSE
OF
SATIRES
Arraigning Persons by Name.
By Monsieur BOILEAU.

When first I publish'd my Satires, I was thoroughly prepar'd for that Noise and Tumult which the Impression of my Book has rais'd upon *Parnassus.* I knew that the Tribe of Poets, and above all, Bad Poets, are a People ready to take fire; and that Minds so covetous of Praise wou'd not easily digest any Raillery, how gentle soever. I may farther say to my advantage, that I have look'd with the[Pg 40] Eyes of a Stoick upon the Defamatory Libels that have been publish'd against me. Whatever Calumnies they have been willing to asperse me with, whatever false Reports they have spread of my Person, I can easily forgive those little Revenges; and ascribe 'em to the Spleen of a provok'd

Author, who finds himself attack'd in the most sensible part of a Poet, I mean, in his Writings.

But I own I was a little surpriz'd at the whimsical Chagrin of certain *Readers*, who instead of diverting themselves with this Quarrel of *Parnassus*, of which they might have been indifferent Spectators, chose to make themselves Parties, and rather to take pet with Fools, than laugh with Men of Sense. 'Twas to comfort these People, that I compos'd my ninth Satire; where I think I have shewn clearly enough, that without any prejudice either to one's Conscience or the Government, one may think bad Verses bad Verses, and have full right to be tir'd with reading a silly Book. But since these Gentlemen have spoken of the liberty I have taken of *Naming* them, as an Attempt unheard-of, and without Example, and since Examples can't well be put into Rhyme; 'tis proper to say one word to inform 'em of a thing of which they alone wou'd gladly be ignorant, and to make them know, that in comparison of all my brother Satirists, I have been a Poet of great Moderation.

To begin with *Lucilius* the Inventer of Satire; what liberty, or rather what license did he not indulge in his Works? They were not only Poets and Authors whom he attack'd, they were People of the first Qua[Pg 41]lity in *Rome*, and Consular Persons. However *Scipio* and *Lælius* did not judge that Poet (so determin'd a Laugher as he was) unworthy of their Friendship; and probably upon occasion no more refus'd him, than they did *Terence*, their advice on his Writings: They never thought of espousing the part of *Lupus* and *Metellus*, whom he ridicul'd in his Satires, nor imagin'd they gave up any part of their own Character in leaving to his Mercy all the Coxcombs of the Nation.

——*num* Lælius, *aut qui*
Duxit ab oppressa meritum Carthagine nomen,
Ingenio offensi, aut læso doluere Metello
Famosisve Lupo *co-operto versibus?*

In a word, *Lucilius* spar'd neither the Small nor the Great, and often from the Nobles and the Patricians he stoop'd to the Lees of the People.
Primores populi arripuit populumq; tributim.

It may be said that *Lucilius* liv'd in a Republick where those sort of liberties might be permitted. Look then upon *Horace*, who liv'd under an Emperor in the beginnings of a Monarchy (the most dangerous time in the world to laugh) who is there whom he has not satiriz'd by name? *Fabius* the great Talker, *Tigellius* the Fantastick, *Nasidienus* the Impertinent, *Nomentanus* the Debauchee, and whoever came at his Quill's end. They may answer that these are fictitious Names: an excellent Answer indeed! As if those whom he attack'd were no better known; as if we[Pg 42] were ignorant that *Fabius* was a *Roman* Knight who compos'd a Treatise of Law, that *Tigellius* was a Musician favour'd by *Augustus*, that *Nasidienus Rufus* was a famous Coxcomb in *Rome*, that *Cassius Nomentanus* was one of the most noted Rakes in *Italy*. Certainly those who talk in this manner, are not conversant with ancient Writers, nor extreamly instructed in the affairs of the Court of *Agustus*. *Horace* is not contented with calling people by their *Names*; he seems so afraid they should be mistaken, that he gives us even their Sir-names; nay tells us the Trade they follow'd, or the Employments they exercis'd. Observe for Example how he speaks of *Aufidius Luscus* Prætor of *Fundi*.

Fundos Aufidio Lusco *Prætore libenter*
Linquimus, insani ridentes præmia scribæ
Prætextam & latum clavum, &c.

20

We were glad to leave (says he) *the Town of* Fundi *of which one* Aufidius Luscus *was Prætor, but it was not without laughing heartily at the folly of this man, who having been a Clerk, took upon him the Airs of a Senator and a Person of Quality.* Could a Man be describ'd more precisely? and would not the Circumstances only be sufficient to make him known? Will they say that *Aufidius* was then dead? *Horace* speaks of a Voyage made some time since. And how will my Censors account for this other passage?

Turgidus Alpinus *jugulat dum* Memnona, *dumque*
Diffingit Rheni *luteum caput: hæc ego ludo.*
[Pg 43]

While that Bombast Poet Alpinus, *murders* Memnon *in his Poem, and bemires himself in his description of the* Rhine, *I divert my self in these Satires.* 'Tis plain from hence, that *Alpinus* liv'd in the time when *Horace* writ these Satires: and suppose *Alpinus* was an imaginary Name, cou'd the Author of the Poem of *Memnon* be taken for another? *Horace*, they may say, liv'd under the reign of the most Polite of all the Emperors; but do we live under a Reign less polite? and would they have a Prince who has so many Qualities in common with *Augustus*, either less disgusted than he at bad Books, or more rigorous towards those who blame them?

Let us next examine *Persius*, who writ in the time of *Nero*: He not only Raillies the Works of the Poets of his days, but attacks the Verses of the Emperor himself: For all the World knows, and all the Court of *Nero* well knew, that those four lines,

Torva Mimalloneis, &c.

which *Persius* so bitterly ridicules in his first Satire, were *Nero*'s own Verses; and yet we have no account that *Nero* (so much a Tyrant as he was) caus'd *Persius* to be punish'd; Enemy as he was to Reason, and fond as every one knows of his own Works, he was gallant enough to take this Raillery on his Verses, and did not think that the Emperor on this occasion should assert the Character of the Poet.

Juvenal, who flourish'd under *Trajan*, shews a little more respect towards the great Men of his age; and was contented to sprinkle the gall of his[Pg 44] Satire on those of the precedent reign. But as for the *Writers*, he never look'd for them further than his own time. At the very beginning of his Work you find him in a very bad humor against all his *cotemporary Scriblers*: ask *Juvenal* what oblig'd him to take up his Pen? he was weary of hearing the *Theseide* of *Codrus*, the *Orestes* of this man, and the *Telephus* of that, and all the Poets (as he elsewhere says) who recited their Verses in the Month of *August*,

——*& Augusto recitantes Mense Poetas.*

So true it is that the right of blaming bad Authors, is an ancient Right, pass'd into a Custom, among all the Satirists, and allow'd in all ages.

To come from the Ancients to the Moderns. *Regnier* who is almost the only Satirical Poet we have, has in truth been a little more discreet than the rest; nevertheless he speaks very freely of *Gallet* the famous Gamester, who paid his Creditors with *Sept* and *Quatorze*, and of the *Sieur de Provins* who chang'd his long Cloak into a Doublet, and of *Cousin* who run from his house for fear of repairing it, and of *Pierre de Puis*, and many others.

What will my Critics say to this? When they are ever so little touch'd, they wou'd drive from the Republick of Letters all the Satirical Poets, as so many disturbers of the Peace of the Nation. But what will they say of *Virgil*, the wise, the discreet *Virgil*? who in an Eclog where he has nothing to do with[Pg 45] Satire, has made in one Line two Poets for ever ridiculous.

21

Qui Bavium *non odit, amet tua carmina* Mœvi.

Let them not say that *Bavius* and *Mævius* in this place are *suppos'd names*, since it would be too plainly to give the Lye to the learned *Servius*, who positively declares the contrary. In a word, what would my Censors do with *Catullus, Martial*, and all the Poets of Antiquity, who have made no more scruple in this matter than *Virgil?* What would they think of *Voiture* who had the conscience to laugh at the expence of the renowned*Neuf Germain*, tho' equally to be admir'd for the Antiquity of his Beard, and the Novelty of his Poetry? Will they banish from *Parnassus*, him, and all the ancient Poets, to establish the reputation of Fools and Coxcombs? If so, I shall be very easy in my banishment, and have the pleasure of very good company. Without Raillery, wou'd these Gentlemen really be more wise than *Scipio* and *Lelius*, more delicate than *Augustus*, or more cruel than *Nero?* But they who are so angry at the Critics, how comes it that they are so merciful to bad Authors? I see what it is that troubles them; they have no mind to be undeceiv'd. It vexes them to have seriously admir'd those Works, which my Satires have expos'd to universal Contempt; and to see themselves condemn'd, to forget in their old Age, those Verses which they got by heart in their Youth, as Master-pieces of Wit. Truly I am sorry for 'em, but where's the help? Can[Pg 46] they expect, that to comply with their particular Taste, we should renounce common Sense? applaud indifferently all the Impertinencies which a Coxcomb shall think fit to throw upon paper? and instead of condemning bad Poets (as they did in certain Countries) to lick out their Writings with their own Tongue, shall Books become for the future inviolable Sanctuaries, where all Blockheads shall be made free Denizens, not to be touch'd without Profanation? I could say much more on this subject; but as I have already treated it in my ninth Satire, I shall thither refer the Reader.

F I N I S.

BOOKS *printed for* LAWTON GILLIVER *at* HOMER'S HEAD, *against St.*DUNSTAN'S *Church,* Fleetstreet.

Two Epistles to Mr. *POPE*, concerning the Authors of the Age. By the Author of the Universal Passion.

Imperium Pelagi: A Naval Lyrick; Written in Imitation of *Pindar*'s Spirit. Occasion'd by His Majesty's Return, *Sept.* 1729, and the succeeding Peace. By the same Author.

Just publish'd, The SECOND EDITION of the DUNCIAD Variorum, 8° with some additional NOTES and EPIGRAMS.

The ART of POLITICKS, in Imitation of *Horace*'s Art of Poetry, with a curious Frontispiece. *Risum Teneatis Amici.*

M. HIERONYMI VIDÆ OPERA OMNIA POETICA, quibus adjicitur ejusdem de dignitate Rei-publicæ recensione. Dialogus. R. Russel, A. M. Two Toms, 12°.

Quintus Horatius Flaccus. Compedibus Metricorum numerorum solutus: In usum Tyronum. Opera & Studio N. Bailey.

The Adventures of Telemachus in twenty-four Books. Done into English from the last Paris Edition, by Mr. Littlebury and Mr. Boyer: Adorn'd with twenty-four Plates, and a Map of Telemachus's Travels; all curiously engraven by very good Hands. The Twelfth Edition, 2 Vols. 8*vo.*

22

A few remaining Copies of Dr. Hickes's Thesaurus Ling. Vett. Septentrionalium. Three Toms, Folio. Printed at Oxford.

ARRIAN'S History of ALEXANDER'S Expedition and Battles: To which is added, A Criticism on Q. Curtius, as a fabulous Historian. By M. le Clerc, in two Vols, 8*vo*.

The History of the COUNCIL of CONSTANCE. Written in French by James Lenfant. Done into English from the last Edition, printed at Amsterdam 1727. Adorned with twenty Copper Plates, curiously Engraven by the best Hands. Two Vols, 4to.

The NURSE'S GUIDE: Or, The right Method of bringing up Young Children: To which is added, An Essay on preserving Health, and prolonging Life. With a Treatise of the Gout, and Receipts for the Cure of that Distemper. By an Eminent Physician, 8*vo*.

POMONA: Or, The Fruit-Garden illustrated. Containing sure Methods for improving all the best Kinds of Fruits now extant in England. By Batty Langley, of Twickenham.

Thirty-nine Sermons on several Occasions. By the late Reverend Mr. John Cooke, A. M. one of the Six Preachers of the Cathedral Church of Canterbury, in two Vols. 8*vo*.

Where may be had the Spectators, Tatlers, Guardians, Freeholder, Lover, *and* Reader, &c. *Books in the* LAW, *and other* SCIENCES; *with great Variety of single* PLAYS.

THE AUGUSTAN REPRINT SOCIETY
WILLIAM ANDREWS CLARK
MEMORIAL LIBRARY
UNIVERSITY OF CALIFORNIA, LOS ANGELES

PUBLICATIONS IN PRINT

1948-1949
16. Henry Nevil Payne, *The Fatal Jealousie* (1673).

18. Anonymous, "Of Genius," in *The Occasional Paper*, Vol. III, No. 10 (1719), and Aaron Hill, Preface to *The Creation* (1720).
1949-1950
19. Susanna Centlivre, *The Busie Body* (1709).

20. Lewis Theobald, *Preface to the Works of Shakespeare* (1734).

22. Samuel Johnson, *The Vanity of Human Wishes* (1749), and two *Rambler* papers (1750).

23. John Dryden, *His Majesties Declaration Defended* (1681).
1950-1951
26. Charles Macklin, *The Man of the World* (1792).
1951-1952
31. Thomas Gray, *An Elegy Wrote in a Country Churchyard* (1751), and *The Eton College Manuscript*.
1952-1953
41. Bernard Mandeville, *A Letter to Dion* (1732).
1962-1963
98. *Select Hymns Taken Out of Mr. Herbert's Temple* (1697).
1963-1964
104. Thomas D'Urfey, *Wonders in the Sun*, or, *The Kingdom of the Birds* (1706).
1964-1965

110. John Tutchin, *Selected Poems* (1685-1700).

111. Anonymous, *Political Justice* (1736).

112. Robert Dodsley, *An Essay on Fable* (1764).

113. T. R., *An Essay Concerning Critical and Curious Learning* (1698).

114. *Two Poems Against Pope* : Leonard Welsted, *One Epistle to Mr. A. Pope* (1730), and Anonymous, *The Blatant Beast* (1742).
1965-1966
115. Daniel Defoe and others, *Accounts of the Apparition of Mrs. Veal.*

116. Charles Macklin, *The Covent Garden Theatre* (1752).

117. Sir George L'Estrange, *Citt and Bumpkin*(1680).

118. Henry More, *Enthusiasmus Triumphatus*(1662).

119. Thomas Traherne, *Meditations on the Six Days of the Creation* (1717).

120. Bernard Mandeville, *Aesop Dress'd or a Collection of Fables* (1704).
1966-1967
122. James MacPherson, *Fragments of Ancient Poetry* (1760).

123. Edmond Malone, *Cursory Observations on the Poems Attributed to Mr. Thomas Rowley*(1782).

124. Anonymous, *The Female Wits* (1704).

125. Anonymous, *The Scribleriad* (1742). Lord Hervey, *The Difference Between Verbal and Practical Virtue* (1742).

126. *Le Lutrin: an Heroick Poem, Written Originally in French by Monsieur Boileau: Made English by N. O.* (1682).

Subsequent publications may be checked in the annual prospectus.

Publications #1 through 90, of the first fifteen years of Augustan Reprint Society, are available in bound units at $14.00 per unit of six from:
KRAUS REPRINT CORPORATION
16 East 46th Street
New York, N.Y. 10017

Publications in print are available at the regular membership rate of $5.00 yearly. Prices of single issues may be obtained upon request.

William Andrews Clark Memorial Library: University of California, Los Angeles

PUBLICATIONS FOR 1967-1968

127-128. Charles Macklin, *A Will and No Will, or a Bone for the Lawyers* (1746). *The New Play Criticiz'd, or The Plague of Envy* (1747). Introduction by Jean B. Kern.

129. Lawrence Echard, Prefaces to *Terence's Comedies* (1694) and *Plautus's Comedies*(1694). Introduction by John Barnard.

130. Henry More, *Democritus Platonissans* (1646). Introduction by P. G. Stanwood.

131. John Evelyn, *The History of ... Sabatai Sevi ... The Suppos'd Messiah of the Jews*(1669). Introduction by Christopher W. Grose.

132. Walter Harte, *An Essay on Satire, Particularly on the Dunciad* (1730). Introduction by Thomas B. Gilmore.

ANNOUNCEMENTS:

Next in the series of special publications by the Society will be a volume including Elkanah Settle's *The Empress of Morocco* (1673) with five plates; *Notes and Observations on the Empress of Morocco* (1674) by John Dryden, John Crowne and Thomas Shadwell; *Notes and Observations on the Empress of Morocco Revised* (1674) by Elkanah Settle; and *The Empress of Morocco. A Farce* (1674) by Thomas Duffet, with an Introduction by Maximillian E. Novak. Already published in this series are reprints of John Ogilby's *The Fables of Aesop Paraphras'd in Verse* (1668), with an Introduction by Earl Miner and John Gay's *Fables* (1727, 1738), with an Introduction by Vinton A. Dearing. Publication is assisted by funds from the Chancellor of the University of California, Los Angeles. Price to members of the Society, $2.50 for the first copy and $3.25 for additional copies. Price to non-members, $4.00.

2520 CIMARRON STREET, LOS ANGELES, CALIFORNIA 90018

Make check or money order payable to THE REGENTS OF THE UNIVERSITY OF CALIFORNIA

Printed in Great Britain
by Amazon

87228167R00020